African Wild Dogs
For Kids

Amazing Animal Books
For Young Readers

By Rachel Smith

Mendon Cottage Books

JD-Biz Publishing

Download Free Books!
http://MendonCottageBooks.com

Table of Contents

Introduction

African wild dogs probably have the most obvious name among animals. For one, they are from Africa, they are wild, and they are definitely dogs.

However, just because their name is obvious, doesn't mean everything about them is. The African wild dog, often neglected when it comes to talking about canids (such as wolves, coyotes, and other dogs), is actually a very interesting animal, different from other dogs in some ways and very much like them in others.

What is an African wild dog?

The African wild dog is not to be confused with the hyena, its somewhat better known distant cousin. A hyena is an entirely different creature with different social structure and appearance.

An African wild dog standing on a hill.

The African wild dog, despite its name, does not belong to the genus Canis, which is where animals like dingoes, wolves, and dogs come from. However, it is a canid; a canid is, essentially, a dog-shaped animal. It is considered a dog, just not within the group of the animals most considered dogs.

This animal is in its own genus, Lycaon. It's the only animal in its genus, setting apart from other canids. However, the body differences between it and Canis can be rather small; for one thing, the African wild dog has fewer toes than an animal from Canis. Another thing is that is has less teeth. So, to any random observer, an African wild dog is no different from a typical dog, though there are physical differences.

Other differences include a lack of dewclaws. Dewclaws are a sort of extra digit (like a finger or toe on a human) that grows somewhere up further on the paw or leg of the animal. It's pretty much got no use, it's just sort of left over.

They also tend to have bigger ears, called outsized ears. Lastly, they are usually lean and tall in comparison. They could be described as fairly thin dogs.

African wild dogs are fairly similar in shape to one another; females are only slightly smaller on average than males. However, pattern and color are wildly different. Dogs from different areas and just in general have black, brown, orange, and more colors in different amounts on their bodies. Some believe this is how these dogs recognize each other.

They also have very sharp teeth. In particular, they have teeth in their mouths that have a trenchant heel, which basically makes them even sharper than many canids and other carnivores. They have it this way so that they can eat meat faster.

The African wild dog is an obligate carnivore. This means it must eat meat, and little, if anything, else. A carnivore eats only meat in general, but some can get by on other things or supplement their diets. Obligate carnivores can't. They must have meat or they will starve.

Unlike a lot of furred animals, the coat of the African wild dog is completely bristle hairs. This means they are rough and stiff. With most animals, they would have an undercoat, usually of a softer hair.

The markings on an African wild dog tend to be mostly on their trunk and legs. On their faces, they are generally all the same: black muzzle and much of the face.

As the dog gets older, it loses hair. This hair is never replaced, and so very old African wild dogs may be completely bald.

How do African wild dogs act?

While it has been mentioned that the African wild dog is very much not a hyena, it definitely has things in common with the hyena (and the lion as well). The African wild dog is a very social creature, and finding one living alone is incredibly rare.

A yawning African wild dog.

However, while it does have strong social bonds like the hyena, things are still very different in an African wild dog pack. Ranging in size from two to twenty-seven dogs, an African wild dog pack has two hierarchies.

A hierarchy is the way power is arranged. One dog, or what have you, is at the top, with others at various levels. In the African wild dog pack, the male and female hierarchies are separate. There will be one lead male. This male might be replaced at some point by a younger one, but rather than being killed, they simply remain a member of the pack.

A female leader will generally be the oldest one. These two make up the dominant pair, and they are the ones who usually mate.

The interesting thing about African wild dogs is that, unlike most animals that live in packs, male dogs are not the ones who have to leave the pack they were born in. Instead, it's the females who move on.

It's important in pack animals that not all the animals stay in their birth pack. This is because otherwise, there will be a lot of inbreeding, and that makes for bad genetics.

If one family of dogs has a bad gene, and they only reproduce with each other, the offspring will have the bad gene in spades. This is why some of the pack must leave, and new members must be accepted.

It is very unusual for the females to leave. However, one or the other gender must do so, and for whatever reason, nature demanded the females do it. Females are readily accepted into most other packs. On a similar note, sometimes males are kicked out of packs, but they are never accepted anywhere else.

Wolves, a distant relative, have very elaborate facial expressions. This is a system of communication between wolves, and is vital for survival. Among African wild dogs, however, there are no such facial expressions, at least not nearly to the same degree.

This is because wolves will leave their packs for a long amount of time. The facial expressions are important to re-establish bonds between pack mates.

African wild dogs, on the other hand, are very rarely separate. They don't need to re-establish bonds at all, because they aren't apart for long.

African wild dogs have probably the most puppies out of any canid. A female can have as many as sixteen in one litter, though more typically she has ten. Since packs are not much bigger than that, a female can pretty much make a new pack within a small space of time.

While females can have pups at almost any time, depending on where she lives, only dominant females have pups, and they tend to only have a litter a year at most. A pack couldn't support two litters in one year.

Pups are born after three or four months, but due to circumstances mentioned above, a mother will only have them maybe once every twelve to fourteen months. When the dominant female has her pups, she keeps them in a den and nurses them for the first few weeks.

During this period, she aggressively keeps other pack members away. Since she would kill another female pack member's pups, she's probably aware that her pups could be at risk too. However, once they are weaned and able to eat solid foods, the other pack members are allowed to be near them. In fact, they tend to feed them with regurgitated (spit up) meat.

Once they are old enough, the pups leave the den completely and accompany the rest of the pack everywhere. Up until about a year old, the pups have first right to the kill, always getting the choicest bits. Once they are a year old, however, they behave like the rest of the pack.

The African wild dog is a pack hunter. Since they live in packs, they hunt in packs. They are diurnal, like the cheetah, meaning they operate during the day and sleep at night. The cheetah and the African wild dog are some of the only diurnal predators in Africa. Many others are either nocturnal or crepuscular, which are two different times to operate. Nocturnal means nighttime, and crepuscular means dusk and dawn type of times.

Hunting for the African wild dog is vital to survival. As mentioned before, this dog can't live without meat. The dogs hunt in a pack, and this is done in a specific way for specific prey.

Typically, an African wild dog pack will sneak up on prey, and then chase it down, able to run at up to sixty-six kilometers per hour, though much of the running during the chase is not that fast. The dogs will bite at the prey, usually at places like the legs and its rear. This is so that the animal bleeds out.

With different prey, there are different strategies. For one thing, with wildebeests, which live in herds, the plan is to rush at the herd all at once and scare them, then pick off a weak member of the herd. This member is isolated and attacked.

With antelopes, their most important prey, they have to cut off escape routes. Antelopes tend to run in big circles when threatened, so if they make it so they can't, they're easy prey.

Big prey is a much more involved hunt than small prey. With medium prey, it may only take two to five minutes to take it down. With big prey, it might take up to a half an hour. This is very tiring work, so it's only worth it if they get enough food to make up for the energy spent. This is why they don't go after really huge animals or animals like lions, that would be hard to take down.

Small prey is easily hunted and eaten whole. Big prey is stripped, meat and organs, while the rest is left behind.

As mentioned before, the African wild dog is a very fast eater. A pack of them can eat a Thompson's gazelle in under fifteen minutes.

African wild dogs are very good hunters. They have a very high success rate, meaning that eighty percent of their hunts end in kills. Only about ten percent of a lion's hunts end in kills, for comparison.

Where did African wild dogs come from?

Not a ton is known about the evolutionary history of African wild dogs.

An African wild dog.

African wild dogs' history is clouded in mystery. We have very few fossils to go off of, and what little fossils seem to be related are hotly debated by paleontologists.

In the beginning, the African wild dog was classified as a hyena, because the animal scientist had very little understanding of it or hyenas. Hyenas were poorly understood at the time, and so were many African creatures.

Most of the animals they've tried to trace its ancestry back to have been on the basis of a lack of a dewclaw, as previously mentioned. However, it seems this lack of a dewclaw is a very misleading thing to use as a basis. It seems like the ancestor of the African wild dog may have had a dewclaw at one point.

The biggest problem with most of the suggested ancestors is that they have very different teeth. Many zoologists think we might not have even found the African wild dog's ancestor yet.

Teeth are incredibly important for identification, and in animals, they take a very long time to change (like many thousands of years). The teeth are adapted for the animal's life style and survival. For instance, cows have more flat teeth and plenty of molars.

Sharks, on the other hand, have all jagged teeth, and a lot of them. Unlike cows, which are made to slowly chew grass and such all day, sharks are made to tear into things.

Similarly, an African wild dog's teeth are made to be the best at not only taking down antelopes, their main prey, but also at eating fast. So, it would be expected that an ancestor would have similar teeth.

However, we just don't know for sure how all of that works out.

The history of African wild dogs and humans

African wild dogs have been known to written history for a very long time. Far back in the 3rd century and possibly earlier, an animal that sounds a lot like it was described by writers.

A pair of African wild dogs.

However, to the Western world, the African wild dog was unknown until about 1820. This was when it was first identified by a scientist who ended up with a specimen that had been taken from Mozambique. However, this scientist had little idea what he was doing, and he was the one who named it a hyena.

Only seven years later, another man corrected his mistake and named the African wild dog a canid. It was grouped with other canids and studied, though very little was known about it for a long time.

It's also known as the Cape hunting dog, the painted lycaon, and the painted wolf or dog. This has been pushed more in recent times by people who want to preserve it, because 'wild dog' has a sort of bad sound to it. Painted dog might be a much better name, but African wild dog is what has stuck, and it's probably the name it will have for a very, very long time.

In Ancient Egypt, early on, the African wild dog represented a sort of cross between civilization and wilderness. It was commonly on cosmetic palettes (which were used to mix makeup) and other things. However, it seems its role was taken over by the wolf, and later on in Ancient Egyptian society, seems to have been largely ignored.

Earlier peoples tended to wear their tails. Some people think that this is because they saw the African wild dog as a very strong hunter, and this would give them the strength to take on their own prey. Hunting was a very big deal in these societies, so it makes sense that they would glorify a hunting animal.

The San people of Southern Africa probably most prominently feature the African wild dog in their culture.

In one of their stories, it represents death. The story goes that the hare refused to let all animals be reborn, thereby making the moon angry. So, it sent the African wild dog after the hare, and the hare was killed by it. This is the story of how death was introduced into the world.

Another story tells of men being turned into African wild dogs and sent to attack other gods as punishment; however, we don't know who wins this battle at all.

They see the African wild dog as the absolute best hunter. So, hunters of the San people would traditionally smear their feet with some sort of African wild dog bodily fluid, believing it would make them as smart and fast.

However, interestingly, despite this prominence in San culture, the African wild dog is very rarely in their artwork.

The African wild dog is considered endangered. It is extinct in several countries.

Subspecies of African wild dogs

There are five recognized subspecies of African wild dogs.

An African wild dog searching around.

A subspecies is probably one of the smallest divisions of animals. A species is a specific kind of animal. A subspecies is an even more specific type of that animal. The difference is that the DNA, or its genes, are almost identical to another subspecies, it's just that they look a little different.

The Cape wild dog is the best known, and it was the first discovered. It lives in areas like Mozambique. It tends to have a lot of yellow in its fur, and less white.

The East African wild dog lives in East Africa, unsurprisingly. It is different from its cousin in that it has very dark fur, to the point of having almost no yellow or orange.

The West African wild dog lives to the west. It doesn't have a lot of distinguishing features, but it is still considered different.

The Chadian wild dog lives in and around Chad. It is also a little bit different, though again, this is not all that discernible to the average person. In fact, a lot of the differences between subspecies are not very big at all.

The Somali wild dog is the last one, and it tends to be smaller and have weaker teeth. It looks a little more rat-like than the others. It looks a lot like the Cape wild dog, but instead it has a lot more dark colors.

The thing about these subspecies is that they're not completely accepted. Some think there are also Southern African wild dogs, and others believe that such things are nonsense.

The trick is that African wild dogs are very diverse genetically. This means they may have a lot of differences, instead of being nearly the same in every location. This is influenced by interbreeding and evolution.

Southern dogs tend to breed during a specific time, for example, but other dogs breed all year round.

It would seem the African wild dog is most closely related to the dhole, which is an Asian dog. It's also known as the Asiatic wild dog; both types of dog don't have a dewclaw, and have several things in common besides.

Otherwise, as previously mentioned, there aren't much in the way of relatives for African wild dogs. They kind of stand alone, though the great genetic diversity of the African wild dog population is why there are these subspecies to begin with.

Other animals and African wild dogs

African wild dogs interact with a number of other animals. From the hyena to the Thompson's gazelle, the African wild dog has quite the effect on its environment.

An African wild dog eating the leg of an antelope.

There are many animals eaten as prey by the African wild dog. For starters, in the East, the Thompson's gazelle is the animal of choice for African wild dogs.

In other areas, common animals include impalas, springboks, and other animals. Everything from water buffalo to cane rats are eaten by the African wild dog. Some have even been known to hunt and eat bat-eared foxes.

Some kinds of African wild dogs end up having very specific prey. For instance, on the Serengeti they have a taste for zebra, and actively pursue them over other prey. Zebras are not the most typical prey for the African wild dog, but these packs have adapted and changed their ways because zebras are so plentiful where they live.

Sometimes, an African wild dog pack will scavenge, which is not something they typically do. This means they take something else's kill, or eat something they found already dead. It can even mean taking a human hunter's catch from their snare.

The relationship with lions is not a good one for the African wild dog. Since lions are so much bigger and more powerful, they often kill and eat African wild dogs. In fact, lions are one of the main causes of death for all African wild dogs, young and old alike. Wherever there are a lot of lions, there are less African wild dogs, and wherever there is a small number of lions, the African wild dogs thrive.

In very rare cases, African wild dogs have been known to attack and kill wounded or very weak lions.

The relationship with hyenas is a bit more complicated. Hyenas were mistaken to be related to the African wild dog, but they are definitely far apart in many ways.

A single hyena may sneak up to a wild dog kill and try to get away with some meat; often, they will be mobbed by the African wild dogs.

However, sometimes hyenas work in groups, and in these cases they sometimes make away with the entire kill. The reason they don't always, though, is because the African wild dogs work together as a team, and have an advantage over the hyenas, who really don't work together well at all.

Conclusion

African wild dogs are some of the lesser known African animals. However, they are certainly interesting and attractive creatures.

Like many animals throughout the world, the African wild dog is in danger of disappearing. Hopefully, it will not be the same as with other animals who have become extinct in the past.

Author Bio

Rachel Smith is a young author who enjoys animals. Once, she had a rabbit who was very nervous, and chewed through her leash and tried to escape. She's also had several pet mice, who were the funniest little animals to watch. She lives in Ohio with her family and writes in her spare time.

Top Ten Dog Breeds For Kids
Amazing Animal Books For Young Readers
Klaria Bennett & John Davidson

German Shepherds
Dog Books for Kids
K. Bennett

Bulldogs

Dog Books for Kids
K. Bennett

Dachshund

Dog Books for Kids
K. Bennett

Labrador Retrievers

Poodles

Dog Books for Kids
K. Bennett

Dog Books for Kids
K. Bennett

Rottweilers

Dog Books for Kids
K. Bennett

Boxers

Dog Books for Kids
K. Bennett

Golden Retrievers

Dog Books for Kids
K. Bennett

Puppies
Dog Books For Kids

Amazing Animal Books
By John Davidson

Beagles

Dog Books for Kids
K. Bennett

Yorkshire Terriers

Dog Books for Kids
K. Bennett

Dogs
Top Ten Dog Breeds For Kids

Amazing Animal Books
For Young Readers
Zahra Jazeel & John Davidson

Cats For Kids

Amazing Animal Books
For Young Readers
K. Bennett & John Davidson

Foxes For Kids

Amazing Animal Books
For Young Readers
Zahra Jazeel & John Davidson

Wolves For Kids

Amazing Animal Books
For Young Readers
By John Davidson and Virginia Fidler

Our books are available at

1. Amazon.com

2. Barnes and Noble

3. Itunes

4. Kobo

5. Smashwords

6. Google Play Books

Download Free Books!
http://MendonCottageBooks.com

Publisher

JD-Biz Corp

P O Box 374

Mendon, Utah 84325

http://www.jd-biz.com/

Mendon Cottage Books

P O Box 374, Mendon Utah 84325

Made in the USA
Las Vegas, NV
06 February 2023

67016109R00021